CRISIS MANAGEMENT

or

TWO WEEKS WITHOUT A WIFE

By Anthony Heller

authorHOUSE®

AuthorHouse™ UK Ltd.
500 Avebury Boulevard
Central Milton Keynes, MK9 2BE
www.authorhouse.co.uk
Phone: 08001974150

© 2011 Anthony Heller. All rights reserved.

No part of this book may be reproduced, stored in a retrieval system, or transmitted by any means without the written permission of the author.

First published by AuthorHouse 7/25/2011

ISBN: 978-1-4567-7719-7 (sc)

Registered with the IP Rights Office Copyright Registration Service
Ref: 293868307

This book is printed on acid-free paper.

Because of the dynamic nature of the Internet, any web addresses or links contained in this book may have changed since publication and may no longer be valid. The views expressed in this work are solely those of the author and do not necessarily reflect the views of the publisher, and the publisher hereby disclaims any responsibility for them.

This book is dedicated to my current wife without whose absence it would never have been written and to her sister Prinia.

DISCLAIMER

This is not a book on healthy eating. Use of my recipes may well shorten your life. In an overcrowded world this should be seen as a public service. The following symptoms should be ignored: indigestion, headaches, giddiness and fatigue.

CRISIS MANAGEMENT

or

TWO WEEKS WITHOUT A WIFE

My wife plans to leave me shortly to spend two weeks with her frail older sister in New Zealand. Other men may find themselves in an analogous situation and I hope this book will comfort and assist them through a stressful time.

I start with the preplanning stage and mental preparation for what is to follow. Firstly prepare yourself spiritually and steel yourself against the slough of despond. Assume an air of quiet confidence and even amusement at the thought that you may find yourself in some difficulty. Before friends and especially your wife, ridicule the idea that such practicalities as shopping, cooking, household duties, secretarial work or finding out why there is no hot water will in any way interrupt the smooth and creative passage of your life. Before your wife leaves ask casually, pretending not to be serious, where such things as the oven, dishwasher, washing machine, drier, refrigerator and freezer are to be found. Check that you know how to open them. Of secondary importance are the boiler, fuse panel and water mains, emergency telephone numbers viz. police, ambulance and fire brigade. More complex and only for the technically minded are computers, fax machines, scanners and copiers. You will already know how to operate the television. Forget about recording programmes. If you are unable to record her favourite programmes, blame it on power cuts. The location of crockery, cutlery, pots and pans and clean towels must be ascertained before you can face the future confidently. Above all do not panic. Remember you have been master of your house for many years and have made all the large and important decisions.

Do not burden yourself with animals. At the very least they need feeding, perhaps exercising and attending to their toilet needs. A conscientious owner will also groom them daily and should study their droppings. You will have to remove hair from furniture and clothes if you keep a hairy animal, feathers if a bird or scales if a snake. Although these creatures are a heart-warming part of your lives, you must part with them secretly. I would never advise any dissimulation but here a white lie may be essential but be warned, recent research at the Tavistock Clinic following Kleinian methodology has shown that wives have an inbuilt lie-detection system, far more sensitive than anything known to the security services. Excellent kennels, catteries and birderies exist, all run by dotty, dedicated animal-lovers who are far more capable than you. The day before your wife returns these fortunate creatures may be collected. They will be well-groomed and gleaming with health and happiness. Your prestige will have risen if it is thought their condition is due to your loving care.

We now come to the sticky part, actually managing the house and your own well-being and possibly sanity. Excellent psychotherapists exist but they are expensive and can never cook, existing mainly on lightly steamed lettuce and windfall fruit. Avoid them. Highly skilled housekeepers and cooks can be hired through agencies advertised in 'The Lady'. They are not for you. The bed will be made as an exhibition piece with hospital corners and starched sheets. They are to be photographed but cannot be slept in. Your meals will be perfection, minor works of art but far too rich to be enjoyed and totally ruined if you are two minutes late.

There are three ways of ensuring you do not waste away. The first is to eat with friends who will certainly invite you, together with a hopeful widow or divorcee. You will have to take presents and converse or listen. Use these invitations sparingly, one does not wish to fritter away one's freedom.

The second is to eat in restaurants which is expensive. If alone it is boring and if with a guest or so, even more expensive.

The third is to cook. The time will come when it happens and one is unwifed. Freedom but possibly starvation awaits the unprepared. I have been given a book of so-called basic cooking and it is useless. Cookbooks are written as entertainment, not for instruction. As a young man I found a real cookbook and cooked and indeed entertained in a minute bed-sit in London with only a gas ring and wash hand basin. I ate and lived like a prince, but memory is not always accurate and it was nearly sixty years ago.

Here is my offer of succour.

RECIPE 1

BREAKFAST 1

A decent breakfast starts the day well. I recommend cornflakes with milk added. As liquid I advise fruit juice from a carton. This makes the minimum amount of mess. If after some days, you become bored, try sliced fruit and yoghurt; even a boiled egg with buttered strips of toast called soldiers, or perhaps ham and eggs. Americans eat hominy grits, squirrel stew, hamburgers and pumpkin pie and where do you find finer, better fed physical specimens. I consider Wyatt Earp, Geronimo and Mike Tyson as splendid examples of the human race.

I studied chemistry at school up to the age of twelve when I was evacuated to the country and then studied girls. We were taught to write up every experiment as follows. This was before the hateful days of Health and Safety. A certain amount of natural wastage was expected and kept class sizes to an acceptable level.

EXPERIMENT: e.g. Making T.N.T.

APPARATUS

The chemistry master said "two p's". I understood him to mean 2 peas which I dutifully wrote down and had my ears boxed for trying to be funny; I have remained serious ever since. The concept was sound; listing everything you need (not boxing ears) before you start.

INGREDIENTS

Include everything and remember the military dictum: 'Time spent on Reconnaissance is Never Wasted'. It is easy to overlook obvious things like condiments, mustard or chopped parsley.

METHOD

Estimate time needed and double it. You will not savour and enjoy your meal if you are famished, pale and spiteful.

RESULT

It may be prudent to encrypt this. Do not send it by mail; it could fall into the wrong hands. It is an established British tradition that classified information on laptops or C.D.'s disappears.

CONCLUSION

Avoid school report language such as 'Could do Better' or 'Must try Harder'.

Here is an example:-

EXPERIMENT: Boiled Egg

APPARATUS

Saucepan— not too large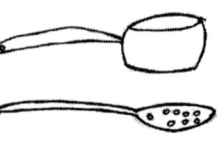

Large spoon with holes in it

Egg cup

Teaspoon

Gadget for taking top off egg

2 plates, knife, napkin

Egg piercer

Timer or watch with second hand

INGREDIENTS

1 or 2 Eggs
Bread
Butter

Take egg and butter out of fridge half an hour before you need it. It is better not to keep eggs in a fridge. Some people keep chickens and enjoy better eggs than can be bought. This involves some time and work. Chicken owners' conversation is severely limited and bores non-chicken keepers. Grudgingly I have to admit that home-produced eggs are out of this world and hens are astonishingly good company. If you forget both put egg into bowl of luke warm water for 10 minutes or so, just to bring it up to room temperature.

METHOD I

Boil water in saucepan and add some salt. Make hole in egg with egg piercer or needle. If you have neither do not improvise with centre punch, cold chisel, paper knife or electric drill – abort mission. The tiny hole will prevent the egg from exploding in the saucepan. Use large spoon with holes in it to lower egg gingerly into boiling water. Water may cease to boil for a moment. Start timer and set for 4 minutes for soft boiled large egg at room temperature.

Check altitude. The reason for this will be dealt with later. Put sliced bread into toaster or under grill, turn over when golden brown. Lay table as required. Remove egg from saucepan using leaky spoon and place in egg cup. Chop top off egg with gadget or axe. If you don't it will go on cooking and be horrible. The soldiers may be dipped into the egg and eaten. This should bring back memories of childhood and is called infantilism.

METHOD II

This was suggested by a genuine French woman who laughed rather rudely at Method One.

My mother said foreigners were clever so I give it space.

Put egg into saucepan of cold water and see if it sinks. If it floats, start again with another egg and continue until egg sinks. Heat water until it boils (bubbles) and time exactly three minutes. This woman (Mme. Escoffier) claims it will not burst even unpricked. Try it if you wish but the timing is less reliable. Always take note of your height above sea level. Water boils at a lower temperature at higher altitudes. Intrepid mountaineers have often had to put up with runny eggs as well as frostbite and altitude sickness. Sir Edmond Hillary and Sherpa Tensing had words over this during the first ascent of Mount Everest. Spread butter on warm toast (delightful aroma) and slice into strips. Sit down and eat well with tea or coffee.

Add RESULT AND CONCLUSION for disciples of my system.

BREAKFAST 2

This takes longer but if you have the time it will lessen the urgency to make lunch and mitigate the need for elevenses.

EXPERIMENT: Bacon or Ham and Eggs

APPARATUS

Frying pan
Paddle
2 Cups
Knife
Absorbent kitchen paper
2 Plates

INGREDIENTS

2 Eggs
Bacon or Ham (both taste better with fat on them
Oil
Butter
Bread

METHOD

Heat 2 plates in oven (80-115°C)

Break egg by tapping on side of cup and lowering carefully into it. A broken yolk is still edible but not as pretty. Break second egg into second cup. If egg is rotten, discard even if parts of it are excellent. Put a little oil and a blob of butter into, preferably non-stick, frying pan and put on fairly high heat. When oil sizzles put in ham or bacon.

Slice bread and place under grill or in toaster. Check

toast and turn when golden brown. Turn over ham/bacon. When it looks crispy remove and put on absorbent kitchen paper. Place on warmed plate and toast on other. Keep warm in oven. Gently pour eggs into frying pan. When white edge sizzles tip frying pan at an angle and spoon some oily butter onto eggs. Remove eggs carefully with slice and put on plate with ham/bacon. Butter toast. This taken with tea or coffee will keep you going for a long time and you will feel like singing afterwards.

HEALTH AND SAFETY

Although I deplore the 'Health and Safety' culture, which stops boys from climbing trees and girls from sewing with sharp needles, cooking is, by its very nature, dangerous. Extreme temperatures will be encountered which have nothing to do with global warming or the ozone layer. I have suggested some precautions but you may be unused to a high risk occupation. Always have Elastoplast and Burn spray or cream to hand. The sort of 1st Aid Box which goes rusty in your car should not be required and the time it takes to read the instructions would be better spent in calling for an ambulance. This will allow you time to take a whisky and rewrite your will. If your wife has been carefully chosen in the first place, she may well have left you goodies in the freezer. These are worth examining. I found some excellent meatballs in tomato sauce which, tastefully placed on a heap of spaghetti, are wonderful. But caution! Frozen food takes ages to unfreeze. If you forgot to take the stuff out the night before, which is likely, I believe microwave ovens can defrost. As I do not own one, I put containers in an oven of up to 80°C or just stand container in hot (not boiling) water to come about half way up. Check periodically. Do not put plastic containers in oven. Hot plastic smells disgusting. Should it melt, it would be a tragedy and you had better emigrate or take a canoe into the North Sea and disappear. I understand that unfrozen foods should not be returned to the freezer. They will keep well in the fridge for a few days. Ignore sell-by or best-before dates. They were invented at a secret meeting of the Wholesalers Association and a corrupt politician. If food looks and smells alright it is still perfectly eatable. It is of great importance NOT to wait until one is hungry before preparing a meal. This can easily lead to rash decisions and ill-advised shortcuts. Many cookbooks promise a heavenly meal in fifteen minutes which is mendacious rubbish. This is the time required to find a knife and fork, plate, napkin and, of course, open the wine. Stay calm. You will eat well only if you treat cook books with the contempt they deserve; they are written by celebrities for the gullible.

BIG MEAL

The following are serious meals

1. OMELETTE

Eggs are important and you should have many available. Only use hens' eggs; duck eggs are too strong, quails' eggs are too small, ostrich eggs are too large and turtle eggs are protected.

1. Turn on a hotplate and oven and heat plates at 115°C – anyway just heat them.
2. Put on a manly apron. N.B. T.V. presenters dress for cameras not cooking – ignore them. Their clothes are burned after each programme. If you do not wear an apron your clothes will smell and your position in society will be compromised.
3. Take a frying pan which looks like this

    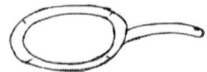

4. Put chunk of butter in it and place on hotplate.
5. Break 2 eggs into bowl one at a time by tapping on edge and opening with fingers or break one at a time into a cup before tipping into bowl. Whisk with a fork. If eggs smell bad start again.
6. Pour eggy mess into hot frying pan.
7. If you have extras, known in the catering trade

as tossafot, such as mushrooms, onions or almost anything – put in pan first until brownish and only then add eggy mess.

Pan must be really dangerously hot. Turn mess over 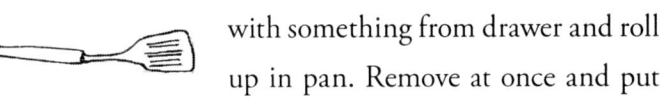 with something from drawer and roll up in pan. Remove at once and put on warm plate. If you forgot, plate may be warmed under hot tap. Add pepper and salt. Eat with bread and butter at once and live like a king. It may well be the finest meal you have ever eaten and you are now a cook. This feast is best accompanied by anything alcoholic, quantity being everything. Push plate, cutlery and pan to one side to await help or return of wife.

Quietly meditate over a malt whisky. This is tiring work and a short doze is appropriate. Animals sleep after eating to aid digestion. Nature knows best. The French eat large meals at midday and survive only because they strike in the afternoons. This is called Industrial Action. The reason why is a mystery like the Holy Trinity and cannot be understood.

OMELETTE MK II

You are no longer a beginner and are ready for a sensational omelette fit to try on ANOTHER —The difference 'Soufflé'.

Heat frying pan clean or not is irrelevant; chuck in a large lump of butter and enjoy the smell. Add mushrooms, onions and lumps of anything non-poisonous and when it looks edible tip into a bowl N.B. Hot butter is dangerous – wear asbestos or other heatproof gauntlets. Now: break as many eggs as you have (two per person if in economy mode), one at a time but keep the egg in the shell. Allow the white sticky part to drain into a bowl and put the yellow part or yolk (rhymes with folk) into another bowl. Take a fork, whisk or electric gadget (I use a whisk) and whirl the white part around like mad.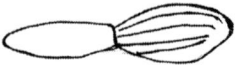
It will become frothy and more solid. This takes time and energy
but is healthy exercise and develops the pectoral muscles, wherever they are. Pour the frothy white stuff into the

yellow bits and stir in gently. Pour into the hot frying pan followed by the mushrooms and whatevers. Pull the edges of the egg mixture into the middle with a paddle type gadget and tip pan so that uncooked egg flows to the edge. Cooking is almost instantaneous. Scoop onto hot plate(s). Sit down alone or with guest and eat with wine, salt and pepper to your taste. It is marvelous and your reputation is established. It is permissible and indeed advisable to glug the wine while cooking which adds composure. This omelette could be followed by some decent cheese and more wine. Coffee will get rid of the giddy feeling and guest should wash up as a token of gratitude. If guest is unwilling say good-bye forever and strike out of address book. Relax with a small malt whisky.

Phone wife, sound tired and say you miss her but are managing. Read undemanding book or watch television.

EVENING

Open a packet of soup with scissors. Yes really. Although by tradition packet soups consisted of salt, sawdust, bits of green stuff and various chemicals to colour, preserve and flavour it, nowadays some are quite good and it is easy to make when you are tired. It will also make you feel a little taller when you discover how hugely superior is your own cooking.

Read instructions on packet; if in foreign language, don't bother. Boil water in kettle. Pour onto contents of packet in mug or bowl and stir. If feeling peckish put some pasta (e.g. a short one like macaroni) into saucepan of boiling water for about 10 minutes. Taste and tip into soup. An early night is advised. As a young man I was convinced that I needed eight hours sleep a night. Now I am no longer young I find I can manage equally well with nine.

SHOPPING

This is tricky. When I was young one went to a local grocer, handed him (Mr. Beddows) your list and waited while he found everything, weighed it and put it in paper bags. Now thanks to progress one must play hunt the slipper in a vast supermarket and always comes out with things one doesn't need (special offers) and forgets or cannot find something vital.

Take a shopping bag or container and make sure you have at least two hours of parking time. Some supermarkets have free samples and all should be tasted. It may be worth putting on dark glasses and trying a second round. Do not try a third wearing a Balaclava. It arouses suspicion. Kindly ladies (employees or not) are usually sympathetic.

In this situation, money is irrelevant. Buy soups (packet or tinned or whatever); bread, butter, eggs, mushrooms. Consider pre-cooked anything but never processed meat. Fish advice comes from a fishmonger and meat advice from a butcher and general advice from other shoppers. Even if you find exactly what you are looking for in somebody else's trolley, do not remove it. It annoys them. Steak, chops and some fish are to be considered. Buy onions but nothing exotic or oriental because instructions are usually in Chinese or impenetrable English. Buy anything in your selected recipes that you cannot find at home.

Here is another fast and easily made meal. It is good for you, will supple your joints and provide, probably unneeded brain food. It would do well for supper and is quick and easy.

SARDINES ON TOAST

Having made the usual preparations viz. laid the table and opened a bottle of white wine, slice a loaf of white bread into man-sized slices. Somehow open the tin of sardines. Put slices of bread under grill until brown on one side only. Turn over and slosh sardines and some oil from tin onto other side plus some freshly ground pepper. Put bread back under the grill, sardines uppermost, and grill lightly. Slice some tomatoes. Remove sardines from grill and put on heated (remember?) plate and surround with sliced tomatoes.

ADDENDUM: My mother was widely accepted as one of the worst ten cooks in England at a time when standards were abysmal and food was severely rationed. Her one culinary invention was called boiler toast. Water and sometimes in luxury houses a radiator or two, were heated by an Ideal Boiler. This was fed from the top with coke from a hod.

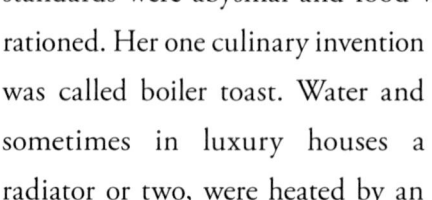

Lumps of hot burned out coke are called clinkers and were removed from the bottom after riddling. Children were used to fill the hod from the coal shed. If they refused or looked sulky they were smacked. Recent research has shown this to be an important factor in the bonding process. A slice of bread was impaled on a toasting fork and held over the hopefully glowing coke. All would have been well but for the invention of a clever-clogs Englishman, Sir Isaac Newton, called gravity. Thanks to him the bread fell of the fork and landed on black gaseous coke. It was recovered and continued to fall several times until finally rescued. The black, foul-smelling coke dust was brushed off and the toast was fed to the hungry children. It was horrible; I speak from memory. Sometimes something was spread on the toast to render it edible. It was this background of home cooking in the good old days that kept me from the kitchen for some 70 years, hence my present refreshing and unsullied approach to survival cooking.

EXPERIMENT: MACARONI CHEESE

APPARATUS

Plate

Serving dish

Large saucepan

Smaller saucepan

Colander

Scissors

Wooden spoon for stirring

INGREDIENTS

1 carton of Béchamel Sauce

3 small handfuls of macaroni. (If you find you have cooked too much don't use it all, just put it in your packet soup

1 packet grated cheese

Small piece of blue cheese if you have it.

1 teaspoon Mustard Powder

Pinch of Ground Mace if you can find it.

Salt and pepper

1 Tomato

About 3 rashers of bacon snipped into small pieces.

METHOD

Put your plate and the serving dish for the macaroni cheese into the oven at 110°C to warm.

1. Cook macaroni by putting into boiling salted water in a large saucepan. Keep temperature fairly high and leave lid off. It takes about 8 minutes. Taste. It should be 'al dente' or chewy. Stand a colander in the sink.

2. While macaroni is cooking, put the Béchamel Sauce into a saucepan. Add 1 level teaspoon of mustard powder, a large pinch of mace and a few grinds of black pepper. Heat gently. Stir. When starting to bubble turn down heat and keep stirring so that it heats through but does not stick to the bottom of the pan. Taste to check seasoning. It probably won't need salt.

3. Take the pan off the heat. Turn off heat. Add half the packet of cheese and crumble in some blue cheese. Stir until cheese has melted into the sauce.

Taste, season if needed. Leave to one side while you deal with the macaroni. If the macaroni is cooked before you finish the sauce, take sauce off the heat whilst you deal with the macaroni.

4. Test the macaroni again to see if it is cooked to your liking. Take macaroni to the sink and tip contents into the colander in the sink. Shake the colander a little then return the macaroni to the saucepan, it dries out too much if left in the colander. Taste a piece to see if you need to season.

5. Smear a little butter round the dish first to prevent sticking and if your sauce is ready, put the cooked macaroni into your hot serving dish, pour over the cheese sauce. Slice your tomato and place slices on top of macaroni.

6. In a bowl put second half of the grated cheese and snipped bacon. Mix lightly with your fingers and sprinkle this mixture on top of your macaroni.

7. Remove warmed plate from the oven and turn on the grill.

8. Place macaroni under grill until brown. Keep your eye on it. It will take 5-10 minutes approximately.

This is a winner and could be proudly offered to the gentry and nobility and even leading bankers deprived of their bonuses.

Following Day: You have earned a rest; eat out or accept an invitation

RECESSION RISOTTO:

This is advanced stuff it requires a keen intellect but I assume only those with a high I.Q. would have bought this book. This dish is quite cheap to make and could be shared with a hungry guest or failed hedge fund managers. It is never-the-less remarkably easy if you bear two snags in mind.

1. Stirred rice turns into stodge
2. Dry rice fried turns brown and then has the consistency of shotgun pellets. It was used to deadly effect during the Indian Mutiny. When peppered with it the poor savages tried to eat the stuff and died in their thousands of stomach cramps.

EXPERIMENT: To make Risotto

EQUIPMENT

Large deep frying pan with lid.
Spoons and usual suspects
Saucepan to heat stock

INGREDIENTS

- 2 cups Chicken stock (this mystery ingredient may be found in freezer or use stock cube)
- 1 cup white Basmati rice
- 1 Onion or 2 spring onions, the green adds colour (to the Risotto, not you)
- A few mushrooms (chopped)
- 1 stick celery (chopped)
- Half a red pepper (seeded and chopped, optional)
- 3 slices of bacon (snipped with scissors)
- Oil for frying
- Diced cooked chicken (buy chicken ready cooked). If you keep your own chickens, first strangle, then pluck, disembowel and behead. This is really a woman's work and it is quicker and easier to buy one.
- Half a small tin of sweetcorn drained.
- Handful of frozen peas
- Handful of raisins
- 1 tablespoon chopped parsley (optional)

BUY YOUR CHICKEN PREPARED AND COOKED. THE ALTERNATIVE IS NOT FOR THE SQUEAMISH.

N.B. Chicken could be replaced with cooked prawns and chopped hard (10 minute) boiled egg.

METHOD

Heat plates. Put oil (cooking oil comes in bottles, motor oil in drums, use the former) in frying pan —just enough to cover the bottom (frying pan's) and heat on hot hotplate.

Fry onions, mushrooms, bacon, celery and pepper, if using, for a few minutes. Turn down heat. Toss in a cupful of rice and stir very lightly to coat with oil. Add two cupfuls of hot stock from saucepan and bring to the boil. Put on lid, turn down the heat and cook for 10 minutes.

Now add <u>any</u> or <u>all</u> of the following, chicken, sweetcorn, frozen peas and raisins to the rice. Put back lid and cook for a further 5 minutes or until all liquid has gone and everything is heated through. Check seasoning. Add chopped parsley if using. No need to worry if you don't have everything, it will still taste good and perhaps one should avoid ostentation. The rice, chicken and raisins are important. Drink any colour wine and taste heaven. Graciously allow guest to wash up or fill dishwasher. Have spare apron available while you make coffee and smooth down bed.

By now there will be a build-up of soiled cutlery, plates and dishes. It is time to use the dishwasher. Fumble near the top until you find a means of opening, your wife will have shown you how but you were probably distracted and thinking creative thoughts. It should be, but may not be empty. If part filled leave and find places for your things. It will do no harm to wash the clean things again and serve them right. The dishwasher contains secret and well-concealed compartments. There may even be a hidden tray for cutlery. Usually in the door one finds a place for detergent (powder, tablet or liquid). Fill and close door. Modern dishwashers are sophisticated and really A level material. Old dishwashers had red hands and answered back. Press all buttons until a whirring noise is heard and we're off.

Send flowers to sister-in-law but do not be too lavish or it will look as though you are celebrating wife's absence.

Phone wife regularly and do not sound happy. Tell her how much you miss her and that you are pleased to be losing weight. Assure her that friends and neighbours are real bricks but you do not wish to be a burden and she should not worry about you. Phone friends or neighbours and accept invitations. Eat out with guest and sneer at standard of cooking.

HEALTH (Excluding Safety)

It is quite possible that the healthier diet and unaccustomed exercise, such as grovelling into low cupboards will cause an adverse body reaction. The usual household remedies should be to hand but might take some finding. Carter's Little Liver Pills, Andrews Liver Salts, California Syrup of Figs, Galloway's Lung Syrup and Elleman's Athletic Rub may no longer be available. Have the telephone number of your friendly local chiropractor available.

Visits to your General Practitioner are best avoided. If he is the usual NHS hack, he will tell you: "There is a lot going about, come back in a week if the condition persists."

"THE BLOOD PRESSURE'S FINE, BUT I'M AFRAID THE ARM WILL HAVE TO COME OFF."

If he is young and keen, beware:

"I'LL JUST SEE IF THEY HAVE A SPARE HEART"

Most ailments of a non-terminal character can be satisfactorily treated by the following good general tonic viz. a hot toddy.

Pour a double measure of whisky (don't waste single malt) into a glass. Add very hot water (put a long handled teaspoon into the glass to prevent cracking), two teaspoonfuls of honey and a squeeze of juice from half a lemon. Stir. Take frequently until cured or past caring.

HYGIENE

Having served my time in photographic darkrooms, I learned that keeping dishes etc. clean was essential to avoid spotty or useless results; nobody wishes to be spotty.

I strongly advise using clean utensils and washing one's hands. When I was young and medicine in its infancy, hospitals were scrubbed, beds were scrubbed, nurses were scrubbed and wore spotless white starched aprons changed daily. Their hair was covered and floors were polished to a mirror-like shine. They comforted you, spoke comprehensible English sometimes with a charming Irish lilt, brought you hot water bottles and told you bedtime stories. The very sight of them brought back roses to your cheeks. Even doctors and consultants looked wholesome. Now thanks to progress, they are glued to computer screens and dress in a supermarket uniform with a horrid clammy disposable plastic apron and creepy latex gloves. At one point medical staff were advised and instructed on how to wash their hands. This is now recognised by the European Court of Human Rights as an assault on their cultural heritage and they smear antibacterial gel on top of dirt and germs; enough to make Florence Nightingale turn in her grave. All the hospital staff is controlled by unseen and unaccountable managers.

If over 90 deaths occur due to lack of hygiene rest assured a review or even an enquiry will be launched, new targets will be set but nobody will ever be sacked. Antibiotics like penicillin were thought to replace carbolic soap. After some years bacteria fought back. Darwin would have known this and called it evolution. The battle against them had been won but not the war. These unpleasant microscopic creatures acquired the taste for the miracle drugs and I advise no-one to enter a hospital unless they are in rude good health. Rumours abound that the present lack of hygiene in hospitals is the result of a negotiated agreement between the Ministry of Health and Deportment and the National Association of Funeral Directors. Washing your hands, plates and chopping board will reduce the chances of your contracting MRSI, Legionnaire's Disease, Food Poisoning, Bilharzia and Creeping Paralysis. I have repeatedly advised drinking a certain amount of wine to control blood pressure. Some of us are happy to drink beer. The brewery industry is going through a difficult time and it is up to us to help them. After all it was strong ale that made Britain what it is today. Drink it with pride. My family did not drink wine. My mother enjoyed a gin and 'It' and my father a pink gin or a whisky and splash. Every year at Christmas time, a bottle of Emu wine arrived from Uncle Harold in Australia. The unopened bottles accumulated for some twenty-five years. After the death of my parents I tried one. I took the rest to an Old Age Home. I never received a letter of thanks. My own entry into the wonderful world of wine was delayed by two unfortunate starts. The first was the very cheap Algerian wine, rumoured to be flavoured with razor blades to give it its characteristic bite similar to that of a bad-tempered Rottweiler. The second was a Greek wine called Retsina which is a by-product of the turpentine industry and is used by the peasants as paint-stripper. During the war, whilst waiting to be called up to the Air Force, I was sent to Nigeria to make a documentary film. My boss and other half of the team was already there. I travelled from ghastly bombed and blacked-out London via Victoria Air Terminal to an airport by a luxury train reserved for the Very Important. I was seventeen years old. I shared a compartment with a fierce and utterly charming Colonel Gordon –"Call me Gordon or call me Sir." He suggested I might share a bottle of Pommard '26 with our meal. "Helps yer sleep, yer know." I became an instant convert.

CHOPPING

a) Some hints on the art of chopping onions and carrots will be useful.

b) Ensure you have a supply of Elastoplast to hand.

c) A sharp, murderous looking knife is best

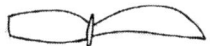

d) Chop ends off onion and cut in half lengthways.

e) Place flat side on chopping board to stop it rolling and reduce number of plasters needed.

f) Make many slices lengthways through onion.

g) Turn onion (keeping it all together) through 180 deg. and cut across many times and that's that.

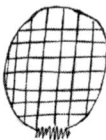

Treat carrots the same way. Take a longitudinal slice off so that carrot will sit on chopping board without rolling. Proceed as for onion.

STIRRING

Use a slight uplift. Do not squash spoon down onto cooking food.

SALAD

If you wish to prolong your life you should eat salad and onions. Onions are a natural antibiotic. They are available without prescription and when taken orally, will cure all known diseases. An excellent salad is made with a sliced red onion and a sliced tomato. Salad can sometimes be found in a supermarket in a plastic bag and table ready, otherwise green things and tomatoes will need washing under a cold tap. If you buy onions you can avoid unseemly tears by wearing scuba goggles before slicing them.

SALAD DRESSING

Salad dressing can be bought in bottles but it is far more satisfying to make your own and it takes minutes.

INGREDIENTS:

A few drops of Vinegar (Balsamic is best, if you don't have it use brown vinegar)

A dessertspoon of Extra Virgin Olive Oil. The name puzzles me I once knew a girl who claimed to be almost a virgin. I am too shy to ask my son-in-law a Professor of Gynaecology to explain. He would probably charge me for consultation. I recall the wise words of my Grandmother "How many times can you be a virgin?"

A little sugar, brown if you have it.

A small pinch of mustard powder.

METHOD

Pour ingredients into large spoon and stir with a teaspoon—then pour on to salad and mix in with two forks. Do not take the coward's way out and use mayonnaise. It may be the French National Anthem but it will not do.

DIETARY ADVICE

Steak is protein. Also important for a balanced personality are carbohydrates or in plain language bread (boring but easy), potatoes and rice. NEVER buy sliced or wrapped bread. It tastes vile and is unworthy of you. Buy a loaf of real bread. Make toast from surplus, feed to birds or throw away.

FAVOURITE DISH

This was a favourite dish of mine some years ago when I was an officer in the RAF (non-commissioned), actually a corporal. It is a treat and well worth the effort. It is also a known cure for melancholia. First find your steak. It is worth looking in the freezer. It should be labelled STEAK and other irrelevant details. Take it out the night before if you remember, if not, first thing in the morning and open wine. If you don't find it you will have to buy some from the butcher. You could buy rump or fillet. Rump tastes better and is cheaper but is slightly tougher. Use it if your teeth are up to it. If possible see that it has fat on it. This improves the flavour and will reduce the chances of a hideous, dribbling old age.

EXPERIMENT: Steak à la Maison

APPARATUS

2 Frying Pans etc.

INGREDIENTS

Steak

Egg

Onion—sliced as described.

A packet of Rösti. This is potato Swiss style and hard to make yourself. I understand Heidi could make it standing on her head while yodelling.

Mushrooms—wiped and chopped, sliced or left whole.

Mustard Powder

Salad

METHOD

1. Lay the table, warm plates and open decent, substantial red wine (better done in morning).
2. Put salad on a plate—do not nibble.
3. Put one frying pan on hob and cover bottom (pan's) with cooking oil or half butter half oil. Butter is excellent for building up your cholesterol, now widely accepted as beneficial. Wait until contents of frying pan are dangerously hot and gingerly put onions in. This is a high risk

procedure. Asbestos suits are no longer available but <u>do</u> be careful to wear a stout, preferably rubber apron of the type used in milking parlours or during autopsies, possibly available at a farm shop, mortuary suppliers or a marital aids shop. The onions will sizzle and turn a most attractive brown. Scoop out cautiously and put on heated plate. N.B. Frying is dangerous—guard against spitting fat.

4. Put in Rösti (read instructions on packet) until brown on both sides, use pan lid to help turn Rösti. Put on very hot dish with the onions and keep warm in oven.

5. While the Rösti is cooking melt the butter etc. in a frying pan, tip in the mushrooms and fry for about 5 minutes. Turn off heat and leave to one side.

6. Cautiously put in steak on slice and place in hot Rösti pan once you have removed the Rösti. It will sizzle. After some seconds turn it over and sizzle other side. This seals it and stops the goodness from oozing out. Turn down heat and cook one minute more on each side. Remove to heated plate to rest.

7. Break egg into cup and pour carefully into steak pan.

By the time you have put steak tastefully smothered with onions, Rösti and mushrooms on your large hot plate, the egg is ready to lower onto steak. It is a crime to overcook the egg or steak. 'Well-done' steak is shoe leather. You will have forgotten to make mustard which only takes seconds. The best is English. Make from Coleman's powder and a drop or two (no more) of water. Stir. The French make mustard in jars and even tubes but yours will be better. Eat slowly using a sharp (steak) knife and listening to relaxing music at low volume. Eat, drink and experience bliss. It is truly wonderful, you can actually feel it doing you harm. It would make an expensive but undetectable way of getting rid of unwanted relatives. Lumps of cheese are handy and could follow your steak. Please remember that nothing comes after cheese except mice. Continentals follow cheese with sweet sticky things for afters. Do not sink to their level.

I repeat the absolute essentials:

1. Make sure you have found and taken out everything you might need, including knives,

forks, spoons, glasses and utensils before you start cooking and read right through recipe twice before starting.

2. Open red wine early or cool white wine in fridge. Check you have corkscrew. If you can't find one in the kitchen use the one on your Swiss Army knife. This type of knife has kept Switzerland out of wars for 600 years and its usefulness cannot be overestimated.

3. Heat plates in oven at 110°C or wash in very hot water. The best hot food is ruined by serving on cold plates. The Greeks do this and a more sickly lot you couldn't find anywhere.

4. Do not use sharp pointy things in a non-stick pan or saucepan; use wood or heat-proof plastic or silicone rubber.

5. Do not answer telephone or door while cooking or eating. Everybody who matters will call again unless they are trying to sell you something.

6. Your alcohol level should be adequate but not excessive.

7. Guests, male or female, should never be invited to share a meal that you have not cooked well at least once before.

8. Remain composed at all times. Stress will arrive; discourage it and treat it with contempt.

SPAGHETTI ZOGERTO

The fourth great wifeless dish is pasta. Here again great reputations can be made with remarkably little skill and practice. Here is my old bed-sit recipe which brought few complaints and much contentment.

EXPERIMENT: Spaghetti Zogerto

APPARATUS

Frying pan (non-stick)
Fork
Colander
Saucepan
Plumb line
Grater

INGREDIENTS

Spaghetti
Pepper
Salt
Pesto (this comes in a bottle. It has nothing to do with pest control and is quite safe.)
Parmesan Cheese

METHOD

1. As always start by heating plates(s) and getting ready a large saucepan 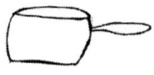 and a colander. Prepare table and cutlery, only a fork is required. I once earned pocket money in an ex-Italian colony called Eritrea by teaching Italian colonialists correct spaghetti eating techniques. It is possible to use a spoon with a fork like the spoon and pusher of a bygone age, but we aim at perfection and this is not for my readers. The trick is to keep the fork vertical, check with plumb line. Have a pepper mill and salt (sea salt is always best) in readiness. Buy a bottle of Pesto, any flavour you fancy and some grated Parmesan cheese. If you can find a grater, buy a lump of cheese (Parmesan is best). Some stoned olives go well but taste first, there are funny flavours about.

2. Boil water in saucepan and add a little salt.

3. Take a small or large (depending on appetite) fistful of dried spaghetti, it comes in long packets.

Do not break it. No gentleman, certainly not an Italian gentleman, would do this. Feed it into the briskly boiling water slowly. It will soften as it enters the water and the water may stop bubbling but keep the heat high. When it is all in, it only needs 10 minutes (see packet) to cook. Taste a strand it should be 'al dente' (chewy).

4. Turn off heat and remove from hotplate. Strain through colander in sink, the spaghetti stays in the colander. If the water stays in the colander and the spaghetti goes down the sink you are hallucinating. Pull yourself together. Tip back into saucepan and add pesto, pepper and grated cheese. This was the exact recipe made famous by King Umberto at his historic banquet with King Zog of Albania.. It is called Spaghetti Zogerto and is now known only to a few high-ranking Mafiosi.

N.B. it is easy to cook too much spaghetti.

This is essentially high-class stodge, it is advisable to have some salad with, before or after it. Eat with red wine and follow with cheese or fruit.

Scrambled eggs can be a creamy delight or a lumpy horror. To make the former use the following recipe:

EXPERIMENT Scrambled eggs

APPARATUS

1 frying pan (non-stick)
Fork or whisk
Bowl
Toaster or use grill
Wooden spoon

INGREDIENTS

2 Eggs per person
Salt
Pepper
Tomatoes, mushrooms, bacon (optional)
Bread
Butter

METHOD

The biggest problem I find with cooking is that either nothing seems to be happening and you get distracted or crises hit you from all directions. Carefully following my instructions will help to avoid tears.

1. Put a plate in oven to heat (115°C)
2. Make toast and put in oven to keep warm.
3. Break eggs into bowl. Season with a pinch of salt

and a grind of pepper. Beat eggs with a fork or whisk until mixed but not fluffy.
4. Put a knob of butter in frying pan and heat until butter melts.
5. Pour in eggs and stir gently with wooden spoon until eggs begin to set. Take pan off heat, continue to stir for a moment or two. Do not allow eggs to solidify.
6. Remove plate from oven and spoon on lightly scrambled eggs.
7. If artistic surround eggs with extras.
8. Sit down, butter toast and enjoy. Once the eggs are cooked speed is of the essence. A maximum of eight seconds should be allowed for optimum results.

You could cross oceans with this inside you, but of course you would need a boat and some hens. Rhode Island Reds are not prone to sea-sickness and are good layers. In an emergency they can be fed scrambled eggs.

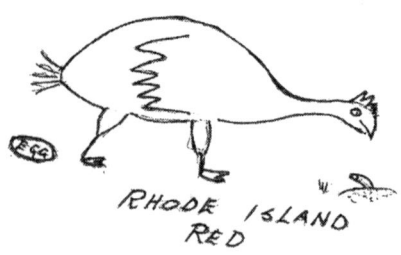
RHODE ISLAND RED

Here is an unforgettable "pudding".. It is quick to make and very, very good.

EXPERIMENT
Rum Bananas

APPARATUS
Frying pan
Fish Slice
Tongs

INGREDIENTS
Ripe bananas (one per person)
Demerara Sugar
Dark Rum
Butter
Double Cream, Crème Fraîche or Vanilla Ice cream

METHOD
1. Heat the butter (one lump) in frying pan
2. Peel and slice bananas in half lengthways

3. Put tenderly into pan and fry gently for a second or two then turn with gadget to coat with butter.
4. Sprinkle with demerara sugar (one tablespoon for two bananas)
5. Allow sugar to melt (just a second or two)
6. Add a splosh or two of rum, slowly to avoid explosion.
7. Remove bananas gently onto a warmed plate. It is vital that the bananas do not cook for too long or they will go soft and mushy.
8. Allow sauce to boil up for a moment just enough to thicken a little.
9. Serve with a good dollop of cream, crème fraîche or ice cream.

N.B. The alcohol in the rum is rendered harmless by cooking. You can safely drive after this if you know how, have a vehicle and a licence and can afford the petrol.

There are a million other recipes. Mostly they are created to be photographed and sold in expensive books. They are to be admired but not eaten. There are cars like this which have nothing to do with transport. There are clothes which are not for wearing. There are even girls like this. Treat all with generous amusement and indulge at your peril.

LAUNDRY

Whether you like it or not the question of laundry will arise. Once upon a time there were washerwomen who boiled clothes and scrubbed with blocks of green Fairy soap; neither survived. The very word washerwoman is now archaic. You are as likely to come across one as a shepherdess or a milkmaid.

You have a number of options:

1. Make sure you have enough clothes to last until wife's return. A large pile of soiled laundry lying in wait for her would get you off on the wrong foot and is unsporting.
2. Tell kind neighbour your washing machine has broken down and the repair man is on holiday. This is a good method but will require gratitude and a present, possibly even an invitation.
3. Every house including the poorest African kraal and melting Eskimo igloo has a washing machine and probably a drying gadget. Any little girl can operate these standing on one leg before she gets her first Barbie doll. You cannot. The risks are formidable. Your socks and underwear will be fit only for the above mentioned child's dolls' house. Shirts will end up as dusters.

4. Proper laundries still exist and are cheap at any price. When your wife returns to a neatly stacked pile of your washing (make sure there are no laundry labels in sight) gleaming and well pressed do not forget to shrug and grin sheepishly. Never lie but mention you think the iron could do with a service.

THE DINNER PARTY

If you have ever imagined yourself leading a cavalry charge you may consider inviting more than one guest; this is called a dinner party. It is a concept both imprudent and even reckless, but magnificent. Always send written invitations; a telephone call will not do. Add a note at the bottom of the invitation suggesting that guests would feel more comfortable formally attired. If at lunchtime it is sound to suggest that it would be appreciated if ladies wore hats. It puts the guests at a disadvantage and renders them less critical. By far the best way is to hire an outside caterer but they must never be seen by guests and must only be used if they are capable of producing apparently home-cooked food containing one or two deliberate but trifling mistakes to add authenticity.

You will serve the food wearing a clean apron over your dinner jacket but a chef's hat would be a vulgar exaggeration. Make sure you know what you are serving or you will appear foolish and will probably be rumbled. Be generous with drinks but never excessive. Only the crudest of hosts would deliberately overindulge his guests. The presents that the guests bring will help to defray the cost. Letters of thanks and appreciation should follow wife's return and modify thoughts (her's) of her own importance.

You will find two weeks of this is enough but on her return wife will treat you with increased respect and courtesy. All this cooking is labour and labour pains are known to be most unpleasant. So for heaven's sake do not dwell upon your independence. You may find it lasting longer than you wished.

There is little more you need to know. With these recipes you will survive and eat like a prince. I have only given instructions for one pudding. This is quicker; buy best quality vanilla ice-cream and a tin of lychees, this with whisky sloshed on top will render guest very friendly particularly if she has held back on the wine because she is driving. If she insists on leaving advise her "If you drink and drive don't breathe, but if you must breathe don't drive, stay the night and breathe heavily." Allow her to make the coffee while you pour liqueurs.

HOMECOMING

Some serious thought must be given to your wife's return. The house and especially the kitchen will not look the same although you may well prefer it that way. If you employ a kindly Mrs. Nobbs, tell her just after your wife leaves that she looks tired and give her the next ten days off. You are better without her. She comes mainly to talk about her ailing children and dying relations. She will also report any visitors. She will need a good two to three days to restore the house to its former clinical perfection and you should keep well away. If there is no Mrs. Nobbs in your lives then find a domestic agency ahead of time and ask not for a "good woman", certainly not for a Swedish Au Pair. We employed one once who claimed to have been studying sex at Upsala University but dropped out after she failed her oral. Request, indeed insist on a professional team who will leave everything gleaming. Guard this secret from friends, neighbours and wife but shyly admit on her return that you have enjoyed the challenge of a little housework but could not begin to attain her standard. Throw out any food she has left for you of a perishable nature. Remove your shoes before entering house and allow no-one else in for the final day. Be extravagant with flowers in hall, sitting room and bedroom. Have chilled bottle of champagne ready and if you feel nervous, perhaps even a modest tin of caviar. Kisses and clasped hands are appropriate but tears arouse suspicion. Above all ask about her trip—there really was nothing to say about the two weeks when you stoutly and stoically manned the ship and weathered the storms with quiet confidence but are more than happy to hand the helm back to her. If the timing is propitious it is quite acceptable to have a meal ready. I suggest something that has been cooked previously and only needs heating.

I had found (and half eaten) a chicken curry my wife had left in the freezer and found plenty of my unfinished rice. I made my simple red onion and tomato salad and reinvented a salad dressing tasting as I went. I had half a tin of lychees left over for desert. The champagne was chilled and the glasses ready. The wine had been opened in good time. She was tired after her endless journey. Her night had been disturbed by a snoring man. Whatever modest success I had with women in my youth, I attribute to the fact that I don't snore. Flying is the very worst way of travelling. She was delighted to be home and to see me. Hunger happily replaced passion and we ate my splendid meal. Then she showered and slept and lived happily ever after.

When your wife returns you will have survived. Cherish her and remember King Solomon's words "Her value is above Rubies".

GRATEFUL ACKNOWLEDGEMENTS

M. AUGUSTE ESCOFFIER
M. ANTHELME BRILLAT-SAVARIN
THE ROYAL SCHOOL OF GRAPHIC ART
THE ROYAL COLLEGE OF SURGEONS
GENUINE FRENCH WOMAN
WIFE

SUGGESTED FURTHER READING

THE GENERAL THEORY OF RELATIVITY - ALBERT ENSTEIN
THE ORIGIN OF SPECIES - CHARLES DARWIN
THE ASHLEY BOOK OF KNOTS - CLIFFORD ASHLEY
ENCYCLOPAEDIA BRITANNICA - VARIOUS
EXIT - A GUIDE TO SELF-DELIVERANCE

ABOUT THE AUTHOR

Anthony Heller was born on 15th December, 1926 in London. The family moved to the country just before World War II where Anthony spent a happy childhood living close to the River Thames and a world of boats. Chemistry was a passion at school a subject in which he excelled until the science master was called up to fight in the war. Undeterred he immersed himself into the study of photography. He left school at the age of 16 and entered the film industry. The War was in full swing and Anthony volunteered for the RAF where he spent three years as a photographer in various hell-holes. Later, after a distinguished career as a cameraman, producer and writer he and his wife drove with their four children to Israel where he embarked on a major film. Four weeks after his arrival the Six Day war put an end to the project. Anthony worked as a Civil Defence volunteer and then worked with the Police as a tracker having brought his bloodhound, Magnus with him to Israel. He had a horse also brought from England and started the first riding academy in Israel. He developed a keen interest in dressage. After 5 years developing his riding school, the Yom Kippur War. exploded. His Land Rover was called up and Anthony volunteered to stay with it and joined the army. He saw action in the Golan Heights and also inside Egypt where he briefly returned to his old RAF camp after 25 years.

The family then returned to England and lived in an isolated 400 year old farmhouse where Anthony trained and competed at a high level on his dressage horses.

Anthony's first wife died after 40 years of marriage leaving a big hole in his life. He remarried and with his new wife set up home in Switzerland where they live on a hill overlooking the beautiful Lake Geneva.